W9-CCJ-065

DISCOVERING
THE CARIBBEAN
History, Politics, and Culture

PUERTO RICO

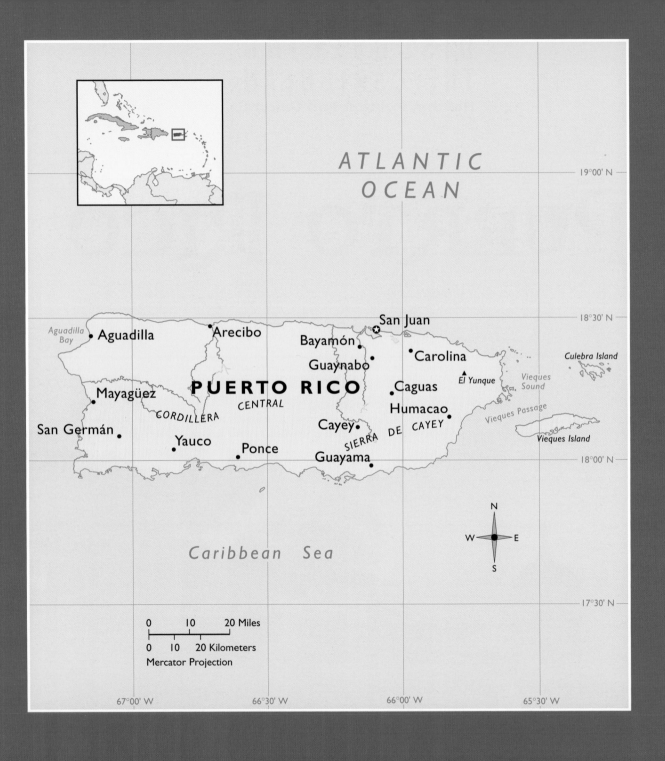

**DISCOVERING
THE CARIBBEAN**
History, Politics, and Culture

PUERTO RICO

Romel Hernandez

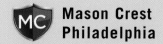

Mason Crest
Philadelphia

Mason Crest
450 Parkway Drive, Suite D
Broomall, PA 19008
www.masoncrest.com

Printed and bound in the United States of America.

CPSIA Compliance Information: Batch #DC2015.
For further information, contact Mason Crest at 1-866-MCP-Book.

First printing
1 3 5 7 9 8 6 4 2

Library of Congress Cataloging-in-Publication Data
        on file at the Library of Congress

        ISBN: 978-1-4222-3315-3 (hc)
        ISBN: 978-1-4222-8632-6 (ebook)

Discovering the Caribbean: History, Politics, and Culture series ISBN: 978-1-4222-3307-8

DISCOVERING THE CARIBBEAN: History, Politics, and Culture

Bahamas	Cuba	Leeward Islands
Barbados	Dominican Republic	Puerto Rico
Caribbean Islands:	Haiti	Trinidad & Tobago
Facts & Figures	Jamaica	Windward Islands

TABLE OF CONTENTS

KEY ICONS TO LOOK FOR:

Words to Understand: These words with their easy-to-understand definitions will increase the reader's understanding of the text, while building vocabulary skills.

Sidebars: This boxed material within the main text allows readers to build knowledge, gain insights, explore possibilities, and broaden their perspectives by weaving together additional information to provide realistic and holistic perspectives.

Research Projects: Readers are pointed toward areas of further inquiry connected to each chapter. Suggestions are provided for projects that encourage deeper research and analysis.

Text-Dependent Questions: These questions send the reader back to the text for more careful attention to the evidence presented there.

Series Glossary of Key Terms: This back-of-the book glossary contains terminology used throughout this series. Words found here increase the reader's ability to read and comprehend higher-level books and articles in this field.

Discovering the Caribbean

James D. Henderson

THE CARIBBEAN REGION is a lovely, ethnically diverse part of tropical America. It is at once a sea, rivaling the Mediterranean in size; and it is islands, dozens of them, stretching along the sea's northern and eastern edges. Waters of the Caribbean Sea bathe the eastern shores of Central America's seven nations, as well as those of the South American countries Colombia, Venezuela, and Guyana. The Caribbean islands rise, like a string of pearls, from its warm azure waters. Their sandy beaches, swaying palm trees, and balmy weather give them the aspect of tropical paradises, intoxicating places where time seems to stop.

But it is the people of the Caribbean region who make it a unique place. In their ethnic diversity they reflect their homeland's character as a crossroads of the world for more than five centuries. Africa's imprint is most visible in peoples of the Caribbean, but so too is that of Europe. South and East Asian strains enrich the Caribbean ethnic mosaic as well. Some islanders reveal traces of the region's first inhabitants, the Carib and Taino Indians, who flourished there when Columbus appeared among them in 1492.

Though its sparkling waters and inviting beaches beckon tourists from around the globe, the Caribbean islands provide a significant portion of the world's sugar, bananas, coffee, cacao, and natural fibers. They are strategically important also, for they guard the Panama Canal's eastern approaches.

The Caribbean possesses a cultural diversity rivaling the ethnic kaleidoscope that is its human population. Though its dominant culture is Latin American, defined by languages and customs bequeathed it by Spain and France, significant parts of the Caribbean bear the cultural imprint of

A cannon from the Spanish colonial era stands guard over modern San Juan.

Northwestern Europe: Denmark, the Netherlands, and most significantly, Britain.

So welcome to the Caribbean! These lavishly illustrated books survey the human and physical geography of the Caribbean, along with its economic and historical development. Geared to the needs of students and teachers, each of the eleven volumes in the series contains a glossary of terms, a chronology, and ideas for class reports. And each volume contains a recipe section featuring tasty, easy-to-prepare dishes popular in the countries dealt with. Each volume is indexed, and contains a bibliography featuring web sources for further information.

Whether old or young, readers of the eleven-volume series DISCOVERING THE CARIBBEAN will come away with a new appreciation of this tropical sea, its jewel-like islands, and its fascinating and friendly people!

(Opposite) A view of San Cristóbal Canyon, Barranquitas, in central Puerto Rico. (Right) Swimmers enjoy the warm bay waters of Guánica, on the southern coast of the island. In addition to its beautiful beaches, Guánica is popular as a hiking area and for the rare dry forest nearby, which has been named a World Biosphere Reserve by the United Nations.

1 RUGGED ISLAND IN THE CARIBBEAN

PUERTO RICO IS a rugged swatch of green in a deep blue sea. The fourth-largest island in the Caribbean—110 miles (177 kilometers) long and 35 miles (56 km) wide—it lies at the eastern end of the island chain called the Greater Antilles. To Puerto Rico's north is the Atlantic Ocean; to the south, the Caribbean Sea. The islands of Vieques and Culebra, as well as some smaller islands, are included in its territory.

A DIVERSE LANDSCAPE

Although Puerto Rico is best known to the world for its sunny beaches, rough mountains make up most of the island's terrain. The main mountain range runs from east to west through the middle of the island and is called the Cordillera Central. The highest peak in this range is Cerro de Punta, at

9

about 4,390 feet (1,338 meters). The native Tainos who lived on the island more than 500 years ago believed the mighty god Juracan lived on Cerro de Punta.

In the northeast part of the island, unusual limestone rock formations make up the island's *karst* country. Underground rivers run through this unusual region, which is riddled with sinkholes and caverns that millions of bats call home.

Puerto Rico is divided into 78 counties, with most of the major cities ringing the island along the coasts. The bustling metropolitan area of San Juan, where about one-third of the country's nearly 4 million people live, is located in the northeast. Ponce is the major city on the southern coast. Mayagüez anchors the western end of the island. Caguas is the biggest city in the island's interior.

Puerto Rico's golden beaches have earned the island a worldwide reputation as a premier tourist destination. With more than 500 miles (805 km) of coastline, the island offers beaches ranging from posh Isla Verde, with its high-rise hotels and *casinos*, to Caja de Muertos (literally, "coffin of the

Words to Understand in This Chapter

casino—a building that houses a gambling establishment.
coquí—a small tree frog that is Puerto Rico's national mascot.
karst—irregular limestone terrain characterized by underground streams and caves.

dead"), a small island off the mainland's southern coast where leatherback sea turtles lay their eggs.

The tropical climate is warm and humid year-round, but the thermometer rarely rises beyond 90°F (32°C) during summer. In fact, San Juan has never recorded a day when the temperature exceeded 100°F (38°C) or dipped below 60°F (16°C).

The island's relatively mild climate stands in contrast to the ferocious storms that sometimes buffet the island during the hurricane season, which lasts from June through November. Throughout history hurricanes have devastated the land, claiming many lives and causing millions of dollars in property damage. The most lethal storm, Hurricane San Ciriaco, claimed more than 3,000 lives in 1899.

Caja de Muertos is a small island off the southern coast of Puerto Rico.

PUERTO RICO'S NATURAL TREASURES

The Caribbean National Forest, known as El Yunque, offers visitors a good idea of what the island looked like 500 years ago, before the forests were chopped down to make way for the farms and cities that began to dot the landscape. El Yunque, encompassing some 28,000 acres on the eastern side

Quick Facts: The Geography of the Puerto Rico

Location: Central America, an island between the Caribbean Sea and the North Atlantic Ocean, east of the Dominican Republic

Area: (slightly less than three times the size of Rhode Island)
   total: 3,515 square miles (9,104 sq km)
   land: 3,459 square miles (8,959 sq km)
   water: 56 square miles (145 sq km)

Borders: none

Climate: tropical marine; little seasonal temperature variation

Terrain: mostly mountains, with coastal plains and sandy beaches along most coastal areas

Elevation extremes:
   lowest point: Caribbean Sea—0 feet
   highest point: Cerro de Punta—4,390 feet (1,338 meters)

Natural hazards: hurricanes, droughts

Source: Adapted from CIA World Factbook 2015.

of the island, is a short drive from San Juan. The diverse plant life in this gorgeous forest is nourished by more than 160 billion gallons of annual rainwater. El Yunque boasts magnificent waterfalls and canyons, and it is also home to many exotic species of wildflowers and plants and the imposing ceiba tree, which may tower more than 150 feet (46 meters) above the forest floor.

Puerto Rico's national mascot, an inch-long tree frog called the *coquí*, makes its home in these hills. But visitors are more likely to hear the *coquí* than see it. The amphibian's name comes from the almost bird-like chirp of the male frog's call.

In recent years the U.S. Forest Service has striven to reinvigorate the endangered population of Puerto Rican parrots that live in El Yunque. The island was once home to as many as a million of these colorful and distinc-

Camuy Caverns in northwest Puerto Rico is the third-largest cave system in the Western Hemisphere. More than 10 miles (16 km) of this vast underground area have been explored and mapped. It is one of many popular tourist attractions in the Arecibo area.

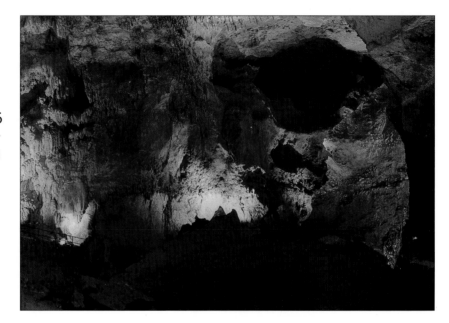

tive birds. But because of deforestation, the population dropped as low as 13. Today, there are no more than 50 parrots living in the forest. In 1991, 16 parrots bred in captivity were released into El Yunque to increase the wild population. Today, there are about 85 parrots living in captivity, and the wild population is growing. However, these birds remain among the ten species in the greatest danger of extinction.

TEXT-DEPENDENT QUESTIONS

1. What two islands are part of Puerto Rico's territory?
2. What is the range of high and low temperatures for San Juan?
3. During what months do hurricanes batter Puerto Rico?

All that is left of the Taino Indians who once inhabited Puerto Rico are relics found by archaeologists, such as these monoliths with Taino pictographs (opposite) found at Utuado. They are believed to date from the 12th century. (Right) Spain's influence can be seen throughout the island; one example is El Morro, a massive fortress built between 1539 and 1783 to protect San Juan.

2 FROM COLONIZATION TO COMMONWEALTH

PUERTO RICO'S FIRST inhabitants may have arrived on the island as long as 4,000 years ago. Little is known about these early *indigenous* peoples. *Archaeologists* even debate whether they arrived from South America or North America.

Archaeologists have, however, discovered the remains of the society that dwelled in Puerto Rico beginning about 2,000 years ago. These people sailed to the island from the area that is now Venezuela in South America. They made distinctive red-and-white pottery and cultivated crops such as cassava, a type of root vegetable.

These early inhabitants came to call themselves Tainos and were related to the Arawakans who settled other Caribbean islands. A peaceful people who spoke their own language and worshiped their own gods, they fished, hunted, and farmed. They lived in villages headed by chieftains called *caciques* who wore elaborate headdresses made of parrot feathers. The highly structured society was divided into nobles, medicine men, and laborers.

The Tainos played a game called *pelota*, similar to modern soccer, in which teams competed in an arena called a *batey* to keep a ball in the air without using their hands. The archaeological remains of about 10 ball courts built by the Tainos 800 years ago can still be seen at the Caguana Indian Ceremonial Park.

The Tainos called their island Boriquen, which means "land of the brave lord." That name has evolved into the modern term **boricua**, which refers to Puerto Ricans. By the time Europeans came, 30,000 Tainos lived on the island.

Around 1400, a tribe from South America called the Caribs arrived on the island. This warlike group clashed with the Tainos and settled parts of the island.

Words to Understand in This Chapter

archaeologists—scientists who study the material remains of past cultures.
boricua—a term that Puerto Ricans use to refer to themselves and their cultural identity.
commonwealth—a self-governing territory under the authority of a larger nation.
conquistadors—Spanish soldier-adventurers who explored and conquered the New World during the 16th century.
Creole—a New World descendant of Spanish settlers.
indigenous—native or original to a country.

A Spanish Colony

Christopher Columbus landed on Puerto Rico's shores on November 19, 1493, during the second of his four voyages to the New World. A chronicle of the journey describes what the European explorers found when they arrived. "Several Christians went ashore and walked to some houses that were very artfully made, although all were of straw and wood; and there was a plaza, with a road reaching from it to the sea.... The admiral [Columbus] does not mention having seen any people there; they must have fled in fright when they saw the ships."

Columbus dubbed the island San Juan Bautista (St. John the Baptist) and the area where he landed Puerto Rico ("rich port"). But he and his men did not remain on the island, and it would be 15 years before the Spanish returned.

(Top) A statue of Christopher Columbus (1451–1506) in Mayagüez. Columbus landed in Puerto Rico during his second voyage. (Bottom) Juan Ponce de León (1460?–1521) led the Spanish conquest of Puerto Rico in 1508 and established a colony on the island.

In 1508 Juan Ponce de León led a group of Spanish *conquistadors* to the island. The Spaniards were particularly interested in finding more of the gold that the Tainos used to make jewelry.

The Tainos at first welcomed their Spanish visitors, but mistrust on both sides grew over time. The Spanish moved aggressively to seize control and easily overwhelmed the natives with their superior firepower. Then they forced the Indians to work in the gold mines. Within just a few decades, the Tainos had nearly been wiped out completely by war, disease, and overwork.

After he had subdued the natives, Ponce de León was appointed governor of the island, which he renamed Puerto Rico. He called the first permanent Spanish settlement San Juan.

Situated at the eastern end of the West Indies, Puerto Rico became important militarily and commercially in the early years of Spanish colonization in the Americas. Spanish ships sailing between the colonies and Spain often stopped at San Juan. The Spanish fortified the strategic city, which over the course of the 16th and 17th centuries would endure attacks by the French, English, and Dutch—three of Spain's major European rivals. The largest and most famous of Puerto Rico's colonial forts, El Castillo San Felipe del Morro—today known simply as El Morro—was the site of many fierce battles. The impressive stone fortifications, begun in 1539 and added to over the years, sit atop a cliff high above San Juan Bay.

In 1598 English troops succeeded in taking El Morro and occupying San Juan. But after just six weeks a deadly epidemic of dysentery, an intestinal disease, swept through the British ranks, and the English were forced to withdraw from the island.

Aside from this brief occupation, Spain ruled Puerto Rico uninterrupted for nearly 400 years. Although the Spanish were first lured by gold, they soon developed sugar, tobacco, and ginger farms on the rich, fertile land. To work the sugar and tobacco fields, the Spanish imported African slaves. These Africans made a profound impact on the island's culture, bringing their language, music, and religion with them.

Meanwhile, the white descendants of Spanish settlers—known as *criollos*, or **Creoles**—gradually began to define themselves not as Spaniards, but as Puerto Ricans. They started to wonder why Spain should continue to rule them.

By the mid-1800s—after the major Spanish colonies in Central and South America had successfully revolted against Spain—some Puerto Ricans also began calling for independence for their homeland. A group of patriots led by Ramón Emeterio Betances (1827–1898), a doctor living in exile in the Dominican Republic, planned an uprising in 1868. On September 23, hundreds of rebels seized the town of Lares and proclaimed the Republic of Puerto Rico. They called on all Puerto Ricans to take up arms against the Spanish colonial government, and they promised freedom to any slaves who joined them (not until 1873 would Spain finally abolish slavery in Puerto Rico). But the so-called *Grito de Lares* ("Cry of Lares") didn't free Puerto Rico. Spanish troops swiftly crushed the revolt before it could spread.

THE UNITED STATES TAKES OVER

In 1897 the Spanish granted Puerto Rico limited independence, allowing the island to elect its own government and send representatives to

Spain. At the time, Spain was in the midst of putting down a serious rebellion on another of its Caribbean colonies, Cuba. The next year the American battleship *Maine* exploded in Havana's harbor under mysterious circumstances. The U.S. government blamed Spain for the destruction of the *Maine* and declared war.

The Spanish-American War ended a few months later with Spain's utter defeat. Spain had to give Cuba as well as Puerto Rico to the United States.

By 1902 Cuba had become an independent nation. But the United States continued to hold on to Puerto Rico. It controlled who would be governor, and even renamed the island Porto Rico (a name that would last until 1932)—despite the fact that the word *Porto* doesn't exist in Spanish. In 1917, the United States made the island a "territory" and extended citizenship rights to residents.

In 1952 Puerto Rico finally became what it remains today—a *commonwealth* of the United States. But just what it means to be a commonwealth is a bit complicated. Islanders elect their own governor and legislators. They control their own police, courts, schools, and universities. In addition, Puerto Ricans are considered U.S. citizens and are allowed to move freely between the island and the mainland. The national currency is the U.S. dollar, but Puerto Ricans do not pay federal taxes. Puerto Rico sends its own teams to the Olympics and other international competitions.

However, the federal government in Washington, D.C., controls the military, foreign trade, highways, and other affairs. Puerto Ricans aren't permitted to vote in U.S. presidential elections or elect representatives to

Congress. A resident commissioner from the island serves as a non-voting member of Congress.

A key supporter of commonwealth status was Luis Muñoz Marín (1898–1980), who in 1948 became the island's first directly elected governor. A savvy and popular leader, Muñoz Marín founded the Popular Democratic Party and was elected governor four times. Probably the island's most influential political figure of modern times, he played a role in creating Operation Bootstrap, a U.S. government program that helped transform Puerto Rico's economy from a purely agricultural one into one that also included industry. Yet despite Muñoz Marín's influence, the longstanding debate among Puerto Ricans over the status of their homeland continued.

Luis Muñoz Marín, the first elected governor of Puerto Rico, was one of the island's most important leaders during the 20th century.

Puerto Rico's Political Status

Puerto Ricans who favored complete independence found a powerful leader in Pedro Albizu Campos (1891–1965). Albizu Campos, a Harvard-educated lawyer who headed the Puerto Rican Nationalist Party, advocated the elimination of U.S. rule by whatever means necessary and was jailed numerous times for his activities.

Periodic violence accompanied the Puerto Rican independence movement. Deadly bombings rocked the island beginning in the 1920s. In 1937 pro-independence marchers and police clashed, leaving 20 people dead in what became known as the Ponce Massacre. Blood was spilled on the U.S. mainland as well. In 1950 two Puerto Rican nationalists killed a presidential guard during an assassination attempt against President Harry S. Truman in Washington, D.C. Four years later another group of nationalists opened fire from the visitors' gallery of the U.S. House of Representatives, wounding five congressmen. And a Puerto Rican terrorist group best known by its Spanish acronym, FALN, carried out more than a dozen bombings on U.S. soil, the most famous of which occurred in 1975 at New York City's historic Fraunces Tavern.

Although it's safe to say that few Puerto Ricans support violent measures such as these, complete independence does appeal to a minority of islanders. A greater percentage favor a continuation of commonwealth status, viewing that as a good middle ground between being a part of the United States and being fully independent. Still others want Puerto Rico to join the Union as the 51st state, and thus to receive the full benefits of statehood.

Puerto Ricans held a critical vote on their political future in 1967. About 60 percent supported commonwealth status. Another vote was taken in 1993. This time commonwealth status won more narrowly over statehood, 48.4 percent versus 46.2 percent. Independence was favored by only 4.4 percent of the voters.

In 2007, a bill called the Puerto Rico Democracy Act was introduced in the U.S. Congress. If the bill passed, Puerto Ricans would vote to determine the island's ultimate political status. In 2010, the House of Representatives voted to pass the bill, but the Senate did not not, so it did not become law.

VIEQUES CONTROVERSY

Another controversy centered on Vieques Island, east of the main island of Puerto Rico. In the 1940s, the U.S. Navy began using Vieques as a base for military training operations, including aerial bombing practice. For decades Puerto Ricans protested, but it was only toward the end of the 20th century that their efforts gained momentum.

In 2000 more than 100,000 protesters demonstrated against the U.S. Navy's continued presence on Vieques. They complained about the environmental damage caused by the bombing, as well as the negative economic and health impacts on the

In July 2002, thousands of Puerto Ricans visited the Capitol in San Juan to celebrate the 50th anniversary of the island's status as a United States commonwealth.

The Capitol of Puerto Rico is located near Old San Juan. The building is home to the commonwealth's legislative assembly.

island's 9,500 residents. The navy argued that its operations on Vieques were important for national security. Although the demonstrations generally remained peaceful, several violent incidents did occur, and many protesters were jailed for trespassing.

In 2001 Puerto Rico's newly elected governor, Sila Calderón, called for an immediate end to bombing practice on Vieques. Some prominent politicians from New York, which is home to many transplanted Puerto Ricans, were arrested during demonstrations that continued through the year.

Later that year President George W. Bush agreed to phase out military operations on the island. In May 2003, the navy halted its programs on Vieques Island. Since then, much of the island has been designated as a wildlife reserve.

GOVERNMENT PROBLEMS

In November 2004, Aníbal Acevedo Vilá was narrowly elected governor of Puerto Rico. However, Vilá's time in office was controversial, and in March 2008 he was indicted by a federal grand jury on fraud and conspiracy charges. In August 2008, additional charges were filed against the governor.

Although Vilá refused to resign his position, claiming that the investigation had been motivated by his political enemies, he lost his bid for reelection. In November 2008, Luis Fortuño of the New Progressive Party won election as Puerto Rico's governor by a wide margin.

During Fortuño's term, the movement to determine Puerto Rico's future regained momentum. In 2012, a referendum vote was held in which 54 percent of Puerto Ricans said they did not wish to remain a U.S. territory. In a second question, 61 percent said they would prefer that the island become a U.S. state, while 33 percent voted for maintaining another type of association with the United States. Only about 6 percent voted for Puerto Rico to become independent. However, the vote was non-binding, and Puerto Rico's political status remains unchanged.

TEXT-DEPENDENT QUESTIONS

1. When did Juan Ponce de León conquer Puerto Rico for the Spanish?
2. In what year did Puerto Rico become a commonwealth of the United States?
3. What happened to the Puerto Rico Democracy Act?

(Opposite) Pleasure boats are anchored off the beach at Culebra, a small island off Puerto Rico's east coast. Once a hideout for pirates, today Culebra is a popular tourist spot. Tourism is an important part of Puerto Rico's economy. The island is also home to large companies that produce pharmaceuticals in sterile factories like this one (right).

3 A Diverse Economy

PUERTO RICO'S ECONOMY is remarkably diverse for such a small island. The Spanish first settled the island 500 years ago in search of gold. The coffee, sugarcane, and tobacco plantations that soon dotted the landscape became the island's main source of wealth. Today, Puerto Rico is home to huge companies that produce medicines, chemicals, and electronics.

The close political ties Puerto Rico shares with the United States carry over into the economy. According to 2008 statistics, about 90 percent of the island's exports go to the mainland United States. And about 55 percent of the goods Puerto Rico imports come from America.

Operation Bootstrap

Puerto Rico, poor to begin with, was hit hard by the Great Depression of the 1930s. To make matters worse, two major hurricanes—San Felipe in 1928 and

San Cipriano in 1932—devastated plantations and forced many families into unemployment and poverty.

After World War II the United States launched a major initiative to make Puerto Rico's agriculture-based economy more diverse. Operation Bootstrap, begun in 1948, encouraged U.S. companies to open factories that would create new, well-paying jobs for Puerto Ricans. In return, the companies received tax breaks and other financial incentives.

At first, most of the firms to take advantage of the program were food and clothing companies. But Operation Bootstrap also targeted tourism, encouraging the expansion of resorts and casinos to increase the appeal of the island's beautiful beaches. Other industries followed.

A Growing Economy

Operation Bootstrap was largely responsible for creating today's Puerto Rico. Puerto Rico's *gross domestic product (GDP)*—the value of all goods and services produced annually—stands at about $77 billion, among the largest in the region. Industry accounts for about 45 percent of that total. Two indus-

Words to Understand in This Chapter

gross domestic product (GDP)—the total value of goods and services produced in a country during a one-year period.
pharmaceuticals—medicinal drugs.

The most modern technology is used at many production facilities in Puerto Rico. Today industry contributes about 45 percent of the island's gross domestic product, the total value of goods and services produced in a year.

tries that dominate Puerto Rico's economy are *pharmaceuticals* and electronics. Major drug companies produce medicines in factories on the island, and computer and electronics components are also manufactured. Overall, one in every five Puerto Rican workers is employed in industry.

The economy's service sector, particularly tourism, employs a much larger percentage of the workforce—an estimated 79 percent. The many luxury resorts built on the lovely beaches near San Juan make the island a top tropical destination. More than 5 million tourists visit the island annually to swim, soak up the sun, and enjoy the exciting nightlife—and tens of thousands of Puerto Ricans provide services to these visitors, either directly or indirectly. The service sector accounts for about 51 percent of Puerto Rico's GDP.

Agriculture—once the backbone of Puerto Rico's economy—today plays a fairly minor role. Just about 2 percent of the island's workers are employed in farming, and agriculture accounts for less than 1 percent of the GDP. In recent times dairy and livestock have replaced coffee, sugarcane, and tobacco as the major agricultural products.

One of Puerto Rico's most popular exports is rum. The Spanish first produced this liquor, which is made from sugarcane, in the 1500s. Today, the famed Bacardi distillery in Cataño processes 100,000 gallons of fine island rum daily, helping to make Puerto Rico the world's largest producer of rum.

A COMPLEX PICTURE

Puerto Rico's rapid economic development over the past 60 years has come at a price. The shift from an agricultural to an industrial economy altered the structure of the island's society. People moved from rural areas and small mountain villages to the cities in search of jobs. Today, the majority of Puerto Ricans live in cities, and as a result there is far more traffic, crime, and environmental pollution on the island than existed 60 years ago.

Furthermore, despite Puerto Rico's diverse economy—the most dynamic in the Caribbean—islanders are not nearly as well-off financially as their fellow American citizens on the U.S. mainland. Unemployment in 2015 was

Quick Facts: The Economy of Puerto Rico

Gross domestic product (GDP*): $64.84 billion (2010 est.)

GDP per capita: $16,300 (2010 est.)

Inflation: 0.9%

Natural resources: some copper and nickel; potential for onshore and offshore oil.

Agriculture (0.7% of GDP): sugarcane, coffee, pineapples, plantains, bananas; livestock products, chickens

Services (50.8% of GDP): tourism, banking, government

Industry (48.5% of GDP): pharmaceuticals, electronics, apparel, food products, tourism.

Foreign trade (2014):

Exports: $68.34 billion: chemicals, electronics, apparel, canned tuna, rum, beverage concentrates, medical equipment.

Imports: $46.9 billion: chemicals, machinery and equipment, clothing, food, fish, petroleum products.

Currency exchange rate: the U.S. dollar is used as currency.

*GDP = the total value of goods and services produced in one year.
Figures are 2014 estimates unless otherwise indicated. Sources: CIA World Factbook 2015.

estimated at 16 percent—nearly three times the U.S. average. Annual pay in Puerto Rico is less than half the national average of about $43,000.

Although Puerto Rico's economy has remained relatively stable so far, it remains to be seen whether this action will have negative long-term consequences. Some companies, for example, may decide to relocate their factories to countries with more favorable business rules and lower labor costs than Puerto Rico.

TEXT-DEPENDENT QUESTIONS

1. What was the purpose of Operation Bootstrap?
2. How many Puerto Ricans work in agriculture?

(Opposite) Puerto Rican folk dancers wearing traditional costumes. (Right) Castillo Serralés, a mansion in Ponce, is representative of a classic 1930s Spanish Revival–style home.

4 Los Boricuas: Puerto Rico's People and Culture

TODAY'S PUERTO RICO is the product of several cultures that, over the course of centuries, have melded to create a unique and vibrant society and a people who pride themselves on their independence.

As a U.S. commonwealth, Puerto Rico maintains close cultural ties to its large neighbor to the north, and evidence of those ties is everywhere on the island—fast-food restaurants, shopping malls, baseball stadiums. English words have even crept into the Spanish spoken on the island, creating a kind of hybrid language called "Spanglish."

Still, although Puerto Rico has been part of the United States for more than 100 years and islanders are U.S. citizens, they typically consider themselves Puerto Ricans—*boricuas*—first. But what it actually means to be Puerto Rican is complicated. The identity of *boricuas* has been shaped by a variety of influences.

SPAIN AND PUERTO RICO

The Spanish were the first non-Indians to settle the island, which they ruled for 400 years, from 1500 until almost 1900. The descendants of the early settlers were known as Creoles, and they developed their own traditions and customs while maintaining ties to Spain.

The Spanish heritage can literally be heard in the streets. Although both Spanish and English are designated official languages on the island, the dominant language of business, politics, and daily life is Spanish.

Although Spanish is the main language from kindergarten through high school, children also learn English in school. The system is patterned on the

Words to Understand in This Chapter

bohío—a type of hut with a thatched roof.
bomba—a drumming style of music that originated in Africa.
danza—a ballroom-dance style of music popular in 19th-century Puerto Rico.
guiro—a rhythm instrument made of a gourd that is scraped with a stick.
jibaro—a country peasant that symbolizes the mix of races and cultures in Puerto Rico.
parrandas—roving musical groups popular during the Christmas holidays.
plena—a style of music using drums and string instruments that originated in Africa.
salsa—a style of music that combines jazz and African music.
Santería—a religion combining elements of Catholicism and African religions.

Quick Facts: The People of Puerto Rico

Population: 3,620,897

Ethnic groups: white 75.8%, black/African American 12.4%, other 8.5%, mixed 3.3%. Note: 99% of the population is Latino (2010 est.).

Age structure:
0–14 years: 18.1%
15–64 years: 64.9%
65 years and over: 17%

Population growth rate: -0.65%

Birth rate: 10.9 births/1,000 population.

Death rate: 8.51 deaths/1,000 population.

Infant mortality rate: 7.73 deaths/1,000 live births.

Life expectancy at birth: 79.09 years
male: 75.46 years
female: 82.8 years

Total fertility rate: 1.64 children born per woman.

Religions: Roman Catholic 85%, Protestant and other 15%.

Languages: Spanish, English.

Literacy rate (age 15 and older who can read and write): 92% (2010 est.).

All figures are 2014 estimates unless otherwise noted.
Source: CIA World Factbook 2015.

public education system of the United States, though there are also many private Catholic institutions. The University of Puerto Rico was founded in 1903 and today has 11 campuses across the island, with 52,000 students. Thanks to the strong educational system, Puerto Rico has one of the higher literacy rates in the region, 92 percent.

The Spanish colonial influence may also be seen in the island's most stunning and romantic architecture—the winding cobblestone streets and centuries-old churches and stone fortresses of San Juan and Ponce. Those cities have spent millions of dollars preserving their proud and distinctive colonial heritage. For example, in Old San Juan (the city's original walled section), more than 400 Spanish buildings from the 16th and 17th centuries have been carefully restored.

TAINO AND AFRICAN INFLUENCES

Puerto Ricans also owe much to their native Taino roots, as well as the African culture brought to the island by slaves. Although the Tainos were virtually wiped out by disease and war within a few decades of Columbus's landing on the island, their legacy remains. Words like *bohío*, the term for the small thatched-roof huts found throughout the countryside, have Taino origins. Native instruments such as the *guiro*, traditionally made from a type of gourd, are still played by folk musicians.

African slaves introduced their native religions, melding them with Roman Catholicism, into a vibrant and mystical religion called *Santería*. They also brought their drumming music, called *bomba*, which is still played today.

New York governor Andrew Cuomo was one of 80,000 marchers who participated in the 57th annual Puerto Rico Day Parade in New York City in 2014. New York has a vibrant Puerto Rican community.

Wearing a straw hat and carrying his machete, the *jibaro* has come to symbolize the Puerto Rican character—proud, hardworking, and independent. He is a country peasant type that represents the mix of all the island's cultures.

These varied influences carry over into the many distinctive festivals across the calendar. Every year towns honor their patron saints—a connection to their Spanish Catholic roots—with big parties. Discovery Day, marking the landing of Christopher Columbus on November 19, 1493, is an island-wide holiday. And in November, the island celebrates both its Taino heritage (with the National Indigenous Festival) and its African legacy (with the Festival of Bomba and Plena).

THE NUYORICANS

A vital part of Puerto Rican culture has evolved thousands of miles from the island. Nearly 3 million Puerto Ricans reside in the United States, more than half the population of the island itself, and they have stayed true to their roots.

After World War II, many Puerto Ricans moved north to the United States in search of jobs. As citizens, they were allowed to move freely between the island and the mainland. Between 1948 and 1960, a half-million Puerto Ricans left the island. Most settled in New York City and called themselves "*Nuyoricans*."

The famous Broadway play and film *West Side Story* deals directly with the cultural clash that occurred when Puerto Ricans settled in New York. Multi-talented Puerto Rico–born actress Rita Moreno won an Academy Award for her portrayal of Anita in the movie version of *West Side Story*.

Puerto Rican communities also flourished up and down the East Coast and in major cities like Chicago. The migration dropped off significantly by the 1970s, but those who came years ago now have grandchildren or great-grandchildren.

Even Puerto Ricans who have lived in the United States for several generations think of the island as their homeland. Many return frequently to see family and to immerse themselves in the sounds, smells, and tastes of their culture.

FAMILY AND CHURCH

The family is the core of Puerto Rican culture. But when Puerto Ricans speak of families, they mean more than just parents and their children. The ties that bind extended families, including grandparents and cousins and in-laws, are strong. They don't come together just for special occasions—these large families live together day-to-day, sharing life's joys and sorrows.

About 85 percent of islanders are Roman Catholic, but the island is not considered conservative. Some people practice the Santería religion, which incorporates aspects of African religions into Catholicism.

Cities and towns across the island celebrate the holidays of their patron saints every year. Christmas is the most festive season of the year. Friends and families form music groups called *parrandas*. They sing as they stroll through their neighborhoods, where they are greeted with food and drinks at every home at which they stop.

MUSIC

Puerto Rico's musical traditions are as varied as its cultural influences.

The musical style of *danza* dates to the mid-1800s in Puerto Rico. The romantic lyrics and delicate melodies of this type of ballroom dance music are still played today. The style's most popular composer was Juan Morel Campos (1857–1896), a Ponce native who wrote 300 *danzas* during his short lifetime.

Bomba and **plena** are two styles of folk music that are often spoken of together because they share African roots. The intricate dance rhythms of *bomba* are the product of various types of drums and percussive instruments. And *plena* incorporates string instruments such as the *cuatro*, a type of guitar, and the guiro, a percussion instrument made from a hollowed-out gourd.

Pop star Ricky Martin attends a Puerto Rican Day parade in New York.

Salsa music is one of Puerto Rico's most popular exports, but it actually originated in New York City during the 1940s and 1950s. The music's infectious dance beats fuse American jazz and African rhythms. One of salsa's founders was the percussionist Tito Puente (1923–2000), a *Nuyorican* who led his popular band for 50 years.

Puerto Rico is deeply proud of the great classical musician Pablo Casals (1876–1973), a Spaniard who had a Puerto Rican mother. The renowned cellist moved to the island in the 1950s when he was already world-famous and helped establish the Festival Casals, the island's biggest classical music festival. A museum in San Juan is dedicated to the musician's life and work.

Puerto Rican singer Ricky Martin started his career in the late 1980s as a member of the teen singing group Menudo. In the 1990s he became a solo artist and scored big hits, including "Livin' la Vida Loca," which incorporates salsa

LA BORINQUEÑA

In 1952, when it became a U.S. commonwealth, Puerto Rico officially adopted a song called "La Borinqueña" as its national anthem. The lyrics were written by poet and journalist Manuel Fernández Juncos, who was born in Spain in 1846 but spent most of his life in Puerto Rico. He died in San Juan in 1928.

With a delicate, understated melody, "La Borinqueña" celebrates Puerto Rico's beauty and rich heritage:

La tierra de Borinquen	The land of Borinquen
donde he nacido yo	where I was born
es un jardín florido	is a flowery garden
de mágico primor.	of magical brilliance.
Un cielo siempre nítido	An always clear sky
le sirve de dosel	serves as a canopy
y dan arrullos plácidos	and placid lullabies do give
las olas a sus pies	the waves at her feet.
Cuando a sus playas	When at her beaches
llegó Colón,	Columbus arrived,
exclamó lleno de admiración:	he exclaimed filled with admiration:
¡Oh! ¡Oh! ¡Oh!	Oh! Oh! Oh!
Ésta es la linda tierra	This is the beautiful land
que busco yo.	that I seek.
Es Borinquen, la hija,	It is Borinquen, the daughter,
la hija del mar y el sol	the daughter of the sea and the sun.
Del mar y el sol.	Of the sea and the sun.
Del mar y el sol.	Of the sea and the sun.
Del mar y el sol.	Of the sea and the sun.
Del mar y el sol!	Of the sea and the sun!

rhythms. He has sold more than 85 million albums worldwide.

LITERATURE

Many of Puerto Rico's greatest writers also held strong political beliefs and were deeply involved with the island's politics and independence movements. Eugenio María de Hostos (1839–1903), José de Diego (1867–1918), and Luis Muñoz Rivera (1859–1916) all were influential political thinkers and activists who also wrote beautiful poetry. Lola Rodríguez de Tió (1843–1924), who wrote revolutionary lyrics for the popular song "La Borinqueña," was exiled for her pro-independence views.

Julia de Burgos (1914–1953), a poet who died penniless at the age of just 39, is considered by many to be the island's greatest writer. Burgos was born poor in Carolina, but she saw writing as her escape. She began publishing poems as a teenager. She was also active in island politics and joined the Nationalist Party, which advocated independence. Later, like many Puerto Ricans of the time, she moved to New York but struggled to find work, though she never stopped writing. She battled depression and alcoholism, eventually dying after being found unconscious on a New York street. In the years since her death, she has become an idol to many Puerto Ricans. Her words live on in her passionate poetry. These are the concluding lines of "Big River of Loíza" (Loíza is near San Juan):

Big River of Loíza! . . . Great river. Great flood of tears.
The greatest of all our country's tears
save those greater that come from the eyes
of my soul for my enslaved people.

One of the most famous Puerto Rican athletes was baseball player Roberto Clemente, who compiled 3,000 hits, 1,305 RBIs, and a .317 career batting average during his 18-year career with the Pittsburgh Pirates.

SPORTS

The lovely waters that surround Puerto Rico make outdoor activities such as boating, fishing, and diving popular with residents and tourists alike. But the island's sports obsession is baseball. And, unlike in the mainland United States, in Puerto Rico baseball is a year-round obsession. During the summer, fans follow their favorite teams and players in major league baseball. After the major league season ends, they root on their favorite stars in Puerto Rico's winter league.

More than 230 Puerto Rican baseball players have appeared in the major leagues since the 1940s. A native of Carolina, Roberto Clemente (1934–1972) led the Pittsburgh Pirates to a World Series championship. He was killed in a plane crash while delivering supplies to victims of an earthquake in

Nicaragua. Clemente became the first Puerto Rican inducted into the Baseball Hall of Fame. He was followed into the Hall of Fame by San Francisco Giants great Orlando Cepeda, and by second baseman Roberto Alomar, both of whom were born in Ponce. Carlos Beltran was elected to eight all-star teams during his career. Today, pro baseball is filled with star players from Puerto Rico, such as catcher Yadier Molina and outfielder Ángel Pagán.

TEXT-DEPENDENT QUESTIONS

1. What is the dominant language of business, politics, and daily life in Puerto Rico?

2. How many Puerto Ricans live in the continental United States? What do they call themselves?

2. What three Puerto Rican writers were influential political thinkers and activists who also wrote beautiful poetry?

(Opposite) An aerial view of Old San Juan, Puerto Rico's oldest city. Nearly half of the island's population lives in the San Juan area. (Right) The lighthouse at Arecibo, built in 1898, was the last lighthouse on the island constructed by the Spanish. Today, it has been restored and is a popular tourist spot.

5 THE CITIES OF PUERTO RICO

DURING THE LAST half of the 20th century, Puerto Rico shifted from a predominantly rural society to an urban one. Today more than half of all Puerto Ricans live in urban areas. The following are some of the island's most significant cities.

SAN JUAN

San Juan is Puerto Rico's largest and oldest city, as well as its capital. With about 400,000 residents, this lively city is the country's center of banking and business. The city's *metropolitan* area is home to 2 million people. The local beaches also make San Juan a popular vacation destination for tourists seeking sun and nightlife.

Ponce de León first settled Caparra, just west of present-day San Juan, in

1508. Some 13 years later, the Spanish picked up and moved to what is today the Old San Juan section of the city. The city's harbor grew into a jumping-off point for Spanish conquistadors exploring the New World.

In its early years, San Juan was a wild city. It was repeatedly besieged by forces from England, France, and Holland. Pirates roamed the waters nearby. To protect the city from invaders, the Spanish in 1539 began construction of the fortress El Morro on a bluff overlooking San Juan Bay.

An even older fort in San Juan is La Fortaleza, the foundations of which were set in 1533. The fort, deemed inadequate for the defense of the harbor, was later converted into the colonial governor's residence—and Puerto Rico's governors continue to live there.

Today, San Juan is a modern city with skyscrapers and fashionable resorts, as well as art galleries, museums, and places to shop. The city's heritage is preserved in Old San Juan, a seven-square-block district of cobblestone streets and 400-year-old buildings and churches. In the Plaza de San José stands a statue of city founder Ponce de León made from the bronze of an enemy cannon captured during a failed British invasion.

Words to Understand in This Chapter

metropolitan—referring to or related to a large city and the areas that surround it.
rain shadow—an area that receives little precipitation because of its location near mountains that block rain clouds.

PONCE

One of Puerto Rico's oldest settlements, Ponce is today the island's second-largest city. It is home to about 165,000 people.

Nicknamed "la Perla del Sur" ("the Pearl of the South"), Ponce was founded in 1692 near the southern coast by the grandson of Juan Ponce de

A view of Ponce from the Castillo Serralés. The third-largest city in Puerto Rico, Ponce is one of the island's oldest settlements.

León. Ponce boasts a proud colonial heritage, still present in its downtown area. Compared with the rest of the island, Ponce has a dry climate. This is because it is located in the *rain shadow* of nearby mountains.

Playa de Ponce serves as Puerto Rico's busiest shipping port, handling more than a million tons of cargo annually. It is the point from which much of the island's sugar, coffee, and rum are exported to the world.

MAYAGÜEZ

Mayagüez is Puerto Rico's eighth most populated city, with about 110,000 residents. It is the main city on the western end of the island.

The city was founded in 1760 as Nuestra Señora de Candelaria (Our Lady of Candelaria), but it became known for the river that runs through it.

A small village on the northwest coast of the island. Today fewer than half of the people of Puerto Rico live in rural areas.

In 1918, an earthquake centered off the coast triggered an enormous tidal wave that devastated the region. Much of Mayagüez has been rebuilt since then. Among its attractions are a fascinating zoological park.

Most of the tuna eaten in the United States is canned at large factories in Mayagüez. The companies Starkist and Bumble Bee both have large canneries, employing thousands, in the city. Mayagüez is also home to the popular brewery Cerveceria India.

CAGUAS

With 142,000 residents, Caguas is Puerto Rico's fifth-largest city. It is also the largest city located away from the coasts, in the Turabo Valley of the island's mountainous interior.

Settled by the Spanish in 1775, the city was named after the legendary Taino chief Caguax, who fought fiercely against the Spanish conquistadors. Located on the road connecting San Juan and Ponce, the area was historically a major agricultural center where coffee, tobacco, and sugarcane grew.

Today Caguas, known as "the Creole City," is an important industrial and agricultural center.

TEXT-DEPENDENT QUESTIONS

1. When did construction begin on the El Morro fortress in San Juan?
2. What is Puerto Rico's second-largest city?
3. What is the main city on the western end of Puerto Rico?

Throughout the year virtually every Puerto Rican community—from San Juan to the smallest towns—commemorates the feast day of its patron saint. These celebrations vary from place to place, but they are marked by religious processions as well as more festive entertainments.

Other festivals are devoted to island arts and culture and to local crops. Several island-wide holidays mark the birthdays of important figures from Puerto Rico's history.

January

Three Kings Day on January 6 marks the visit of the Magi to the infant Jesus. Families exchange presents on this day, a bigger gift-giving holiday in Latin America than Christmas.

January 11 marks the **Birthday of Eugenio María de Hostos** (1839–1903). This writer and statesman fought for independence and the abolition of slavery.

The **San Sebastian Street Festival** in San Juan is a celebration of Puerto Rican arts, music, dance, and food. The event takes place the third week of January.

February

Carnival in Ponce is an exciting, often wild, six-day party before the solemn Christian season of Lent. Partygoers don colorful costumes and scary masks and take to the streets to dance.

At the end of the month, the rich smell of coffee fills the air during the **Coffee Festival** in Yauco.

March

March is the month for the **Ponce Crafts Fair,** which spotlights the pottery, paintings, and other work of island artists. The fair also includes plenty of music, food, and dancing.

March 22, **Emancipation Day**, commemorates the 1873 abolition of slavery on the island.

April

The **Brujo Carnival** in Guayama celebrates the island's rich African heritage. Storytellers spin tales based on ancient legends about magic and witchcraft passed down through the generations.

On April 16, Puerto Ricans celebrate the **Birthday of José de Diego** (1867–1918), a much-loved poet and politician.

May

On May 3 Bayamón, a San Juan suburb, celebrates the **Festival of Santa Cruz** in honor of its patron saint.

May is also the month when Ponce hosts the **Week of Danza**, a celebration of the ballroom music and dance tradition that flourished on the island during the 1800s.

On May 30 Carolina, another large city near San Juan, celebrates its patron saint's day with the **Festival of San Fernando**.

June

Musicians and music lovers from around the world flock to San Juan, Ponce, and Mayagüez in

June to enjoy the **Casals Festival**. Founded in 1957 by the renowned cellist Pablo Casals, who lived in Puerto Rico for many years, the festival has become the region's largest classical music event.

On June 24, all of Puerto Rico celebrates **San Juan Bautista Day** to honor the patron saint of the capital. Music and dancing highlight the festivities.

July

The **Festival of Flowers**, held at the beginning of the month in the mountain town of Aibonito, celebrates the island's rich flora. It features exhibits of orchids, lilies, and many other flowers.

On July 15, Puerto Ricans commemorate the **Birthday of Luis Muñoz Rivera** (1859–1916), a journalist, poet, and politician who pushed for greater independence from Spain and, later, the United States.

The 27th of July is the **Birthday of José Celso Barbosa** (1857–1921), an early advocate of statehood for Puerto Rico.

The feast day of **San Germán**, July 31, is celebrated in the Puerto Rican city of the same name, one of Puerto Rico's oldest cities.

August

In August, San Juan hosts the **International Salsa Festival**.

September

The town of Añasco's **Festival de Bomba y Plena**, held in September, celebrates the rich musical traditions that African slaves brought to the island and that still thrive today. Añasco is in western Puerto Rico, north of Mayagüez.

October

The **National Festival of the Plantain**, held during October in Corozal, a town southwest of San Juan, honors a fruit that's cousin to the banana.

November

Discovery Day marks the anniversary of the day Christopher Columbus first landed on the island—November 19, 1493.

The **National Indigenous Festival** in Jayuya, also observed on November 19, commemorates the traditions of the Tainos, who lived on the island for hundreds of years before the arrival of Columbus. In addition to music and fun, this festival seeks to raise awareness about Taino history and culture.

December

Ponce celebrates **Las Mañanitas** on December 12 to honor Our Lady of Guadalupe, the city's patron saint.

During the **Festival of the Masks** in Hatillo, people dress in scary masks to mark the Feast of the Holy Innocents. Many observe the day by playing practical jokes.

The Christmas season, or **Navidades**, lasts from December 15 to January 16. In many towns, groups of musicians called *parrandas* roam neighborhoods playing holiday tunes.

Arroz con Pollo **(Rice with Chicken)**

2 onions, chopped
1 large garlic head, cloves removed and peeled
1 bunch cilantro
2 green bell peppers, chopped
3 tbsp olive oil
3 lbs chicken pieces
1 cup (8 oz) chopped tomatoes
5 cups chicken stock
1 1/2 cups long-grain rice
1/2 tsp powdered saffron
Water
Salt
Pepper

Directions:
1. Soak the rice and saffron in a bowl for 1 hour.
2. Sprinkle chicken pieces with salt and pepper.
3. Place the onions, garlic, cilantro, and bell peppers in a food processor and mix until well blended. This mixture is called *sofrito*.
4. In a large casserole over medium heat, cook the olive oil and *sofrito*. Add the chicken pieces, browning them on each side about 7 minutes.
5. Add the tomatoes and cook about 4 minutes.
6. Add the chicken stock and bring to a boil.
7. Add the rice and saffron.
8. Bring to a boil. When little craters start to form on top of the rice, place casserole in oven preheated to 350°F for 30 minutes.

Arroz con Gandules **(Rice with Pigeon Peas)**

2 onions, chopped
1 large garlic head, cloves removed and peeled
1 bunch cilantro
2 green bell peppers, chopped
3 tbsp olive oil
1 cup (8 oz) chopped tomatoes
2 cups long-grain rice
16-oz can pigeon peas (*gandules*)
Water
Salt

Directions:
1. Place the onions, garlic, cilantro, and bell peppers in a food processor and mix until well blended. This mixture is called *sofrito*.
2. In a saucepan over medium heat, cook the olive oil, tomato sauce, and *sofrito* for 5 minutes.
3. Add remaining ingredients plus 3 cups of water.
4. Turn heat to high and bring to a boil.
5. When most of the water is absorbed and little craters start to form on top of the rice, turn heat to low and cover. Cook about 30 minutes until rice is done.

Mofongo

3 large green plantains
1/2 lb store-bought fried pork rinds
1/2 cup vegetable oil
3 garlic cloves
1 tbsp olive oil
3 cups water
1 tbsp salt

Directions:
1. Peel plantains and cut into one-inch slices.
2. Dissolve salt in the water. Place plantain slices in the water for 15 minutes. Remove plantains and dry on paper towels.
3. Heat vegetable oil in a large frying pan over medium-high heat. When the oil is hot enough to make a piece of plantain sizzle, place all the slices in the pan.
4. Fry plantains for five minutes each side. Remove and dry on paper towels.
5. In a large bowl, mash together first, the olive oil and the peeled garlic cloves; second, the cooked plantain; and finally, the pork rinds.
6. Form mixture into individual balls and serve hot over white rice.

Tostones

(Serves 4 as side dish)
2 green plantains
1/2 cup vegetable or corn oil

Directions:
1. Peel and cut the plantains into one-inch slices.
2. Heat oil in a large frying pan over medium-high heat. When the oil is hot enough to make a piece of plantain sizzle, place all the slices in the pan.
3. Fry plantains for two minutes each side.
4. Remove slices from oil and dry them on a paper towel.
5. Place slices inside a folded-up brown paper bag and squash them with the palm of your hand until they're about 1/2 inch thick.
6. Fry slices in the hot oil again for 4 minutes per side.
7. Remove slices from the oil, then dry again on paper towels. Sprinkle with salt and serve.

Amerindian—a term for the indigenous peoples of North, Central, and South America, including the Caribbean islands, before the arrival of Europeans in the late 15th century.

cay—a low island or reef made from sand or coral.

civil liberty—the right of people to do or say things that are not illegal without being stopped or interrupted by the government.

conquistador—any one of the Spanish leaders of the conquest of the Americas in the 1500s.

Communism—a political system in which all resources, industries, and property are considered to be held in common by all the people, with government as the central authority responsible for controlling all economic and social activity.

coup d'état—the violent overthrow of an existing government by a small group.

deforestation—the action or process of clearing forests.

economic system—the production, distribution, and consumption of goods and services within a country.

ecotourism—a form of tourism in which resorts attempt to minimize the impact of visitors on the local environment, contribute to conserving habitats, and employ local people.

embargo—a government restriction or restraint on commerce, especially an order that prohibits trade with a particular nation.

exploit—to take advantage of something; to use something unfairly.

foreign aid—financial assistance given by one country to another.

free trade—trade based on the unrestricted exchange of goods, with tariffs (taxes) only used to create revenue, not keep out foreign goods.

hurricane—a very powerful and destructive storm, characterized by high winds and significant rainfall, that often occurs in the western Atlantic Ocean and the Caribbean Sea between June and November.

leeward—a side that is sheltered or away from the wind.

mestizo—a person of mixed Amerindian and European (typically Spanish) descent.

offshore banking—a term applied to banking transactions conducted between participants located outside of a country. Such transactions Some Caribbean countries have become known for this practice thanks to their banking laws.

plaza—the central open square at the center of colonial-era cities in Latin America.

plebiscite—a vote by which the people of an entire country express their opinion on a particular government or national policy.

population density—a measurement of the number of people living in a specific area, such a square mile or square kilometer.

pre-Columbian—referring to a time before the 1490s, when Christopher Columbus landed in the Americas.

regime—a period of rule by a particular government, especially one that is considered to be oppressive.

service industry—any business, organization, or profession that does work for a customer, but is not involved in manufacturing.

windward—the side or direction from which the wind is blowing.

Create a wildlife map

Draw a large map of Puerto Rico. In the margins draw pictures and write short descriptions of at least six different animal or bird species native to the island.

Create a literary biography map

Draw a large map of Puerto Rico. In the margins write three-paragraph biographies of the following writers, drawing arrows to their birthplaces. Make sure to include when they were born and died and their most famous works:

- Manuel Alonso
- Julia de Burgos
- José de Diego
- José Gautier Benítez
- Luis Muñoz Rivera
- Luis Rafael Sánchez

Debate

Pick one of the major viewpoints regarding Puerto Rico's political status: commonwealth, statehood, or independence. Form a team with classmates who chose the same viewpoint, and prepare a 10-minute oral presentation explaining why the political status you picked is best. After the supporters of each position have had a chance to make their presentation, each team should make a 3-minute rebuttal, responding to what the other teams have said.

Flashcards

The Spanish spoken in Puerto Rico has been influenced by the languages of the Tainos and African slaves. English words also have been influenced. You'll need a good dictionary for this assignment. Divide into two teams with five words each. Look up the definitions of the following words and make flashcards with the word on one side and the language it originally came from on the other. Use the cards to quiz the other team about the word origins. Team 1: hammock, yam, canoe, barbecue, banjo. Team 2: cola, cannibal, banana, mangrove, hurricane, voodoo.

PROJECT AND REPORT IDEAS

Crafts

- Draw a picture of the flags of Puerto Rico and four other Caribbean countries of your choosing. Write two-paragraph descriptions detailing the stories of how each of the flags originated and when and where they were first flown.
- Design and write the front page of a newspaper for November 19, 1493—the day Christopher Columbus landed on Puerto Rico. Draw a picture of what you imagine his landing looked like. Write an imaginary news article about the event, making sure to include "quotes" from both Columbus and his crew and the Tainos they encountered.
- Design and write a foldout travel brochure for Puerto Rico. Highlight three or four reasons tourists should visit the island. Use your own drawings to illustrate.
- Find out what El Morro in San Juan looks like today from maps and photographs. Do your research on the Internet and using library books. Use cardboard and other household materials to make a model of the fort.

Reports

Write a one-page, five-paragraph report answering one of the following questions. You'll need to do additional research. There are no right or wrong answers—you should form an opinion and back it up with facts. Begin with an introduction, three paragraphs to develop a main idea, and a conclusion:

- Was the United States right to get involved in the Spanish-American War?
- Did Puerto Rico's shift from an agricultural to an industrial society benefit the island's people?
- What is the best political status for Puerto Rico: commonwealth, statehood, or independence?
- Should the U.S. cease military operations on Vieques?
- Both salsa music and rock and roll are influenced by African music. How do these musical styles differ? How are they similar?

CHRONOLOGY

Ca. 2000 BCE First inhabitants settle the island now known as Puerto Rico.

200 CE Arawak Indians from South America, called Tainos, arrive; over the next 1,200 years they will establish a highly structured, thriving culture on the island.

Ca. 1400 Warlike Caribs invade Puerto Rico, begin clashing with Tainos.

1493 Columbus reaches the island November 19 during his second voyage to the New World.

1508 Juan Ponce de León founds the first Spanish settlement in Caparra.

1539 Construction begins on San Felipe del Morro castle to defend the island against invaders.

1595 British forces under the command of Sir Francis Drake attack Puerto Rico but are fought off by the Spanish; three years later, the British briefly occupy the island.

1625 The Dutch attempt unsuccessfully to seize control of the island.

1797 British forces invade again and are fought off again; the attempt marks the last foreign invasion of the island for more than 100 years.

1868 The Cry of Lares marks the first major uprising against Spanish rule.

1873 Spain abolishes slavery on the island.

1895 The Puerto Rican flag flies over the island for the first time.

1897 Spain decides to grant Puerto Rico limited independence.

1898 The United States goes to war with Spain after the battleship *Maine* blows up in Cuba; Spain loses war and later gives up control of Puerto Rico.

1917 Puerto Rico becomes a U.S. territory; islanders are given citizenship.

1918 A strong earthquake and an accompanying tidal wave devastate the island's west coast, particularly the city of Mayagüez.

1940s The U.S. government launches Operation Bootstrap to transform the island economy from agriculture to manufacturing.

1948 Islanders elect, for the first time, their own governor: Luis Muñoz Marín, who would remain an influential figure in island politics for decades.

1952 Puerto Rico becomes a commonwealth of the United States.

1954 Pro-independence terrorists wound five congressmen in the U.S. House of Representatives.

1967 In the first vote of its kind, islanders choose overwhelmingly to remain a commonwealth.

1993 In another vote on their political status, Puerto Ricans narrowly choose retaining commonwealth status over U.S. statehood.

2000 Sila Calderón is elected the island's first woman governor.

2003 U.S. military activity ends on Vieques Island.

2005 Aníbal Acevedo Vilá takes office as governor of Puerto Rico.

2007 In September, activist Juan Mari Bras becomes the first person to receive a certificate of Puerto Rican citizenship. The document is good for local identification but cannot be used for international travel because Puerto Rico remains a commonwealth of the United States.

2008 A federal grand jury indicts Vilá on fraud and corruption charges.

2012 In a non-binding referendum, 54 percent of Puerto Ricans indicate that they are not satisfied with the island's current political status.

2013 In January, Alejandro García Padilla takes office as governor.

2015 Governor Garcia Padilla proposes implementation of a Value Added Tax of between 12 and 16 percent imposed on all goods and services sold.

Balletto, Barbara. *Insight Guide—Puerto Rico*. London: APA Publications, 2007.

Gutner, Howard. *Puerto Rico*. New York: Children's Press, 2009.

Heuman, Gad. *The Caribbean: A Brief History*. New York: Bloomsbury, 2014.

Milivojevic, JoAnn. *Puerto Rico*. Minneapolis: Lerner, 2009.

Moya Pons, Frank. *History of the Caribbean: Plantations, Trade, and War in the Atlantic World*. Princeton, N.J.: Markus Wiener Publishers, 2012.

Pierce Flores, Lisa. *The History of Puerto Rico*. Santa Barbara, CA: Greenwood Press, 2010.

Travel Information

http://www.topuertorico.org
http://www.gotopuertorico.com
http://www.seepuertorico.com
http://www.lonelyplanet.com/puerto-rico

History and Geography

http://welcome.topuertorico.org
http://americanhistory.si.edu/vidal
http://memory.loc.gov/ammem/collections/puertorico/

Economic and Political Information

https://www.cia.gov/library/publications/the-world-factbook/geos/rq.html
http://www.gksoft.com/govt/en/pr.html
http://www.politicalresources.net/puertorico.htm

Puerto Rico Tourism Company
P.O. Box 902-3960
San Juan, P.R. 00902-3960
Phone: 1-800-866-7827

Puerto Rico Resident Commissioner's Office
126 Cannon HOB
Washington, DC 20515-5401
Phone: (202) 225-2615

Puerto Rico Governor's Office
La Fortaleza
P.O. Box 9020082
San Juan, P.R. 00902-0082
Phone: (787) 721-7000

Page
1:   used under license from Shutterstock, Inc.
2:   © OTTN Publishing
3:   © OTTN Publishing
7:   Photo Disc
8:   Courtesy of the Puerto Rico Tourism
       Company
9:   Courtesy of the Puerto Rico Tourism
       Company
11: Courtesy of the Puerto Rico Tourism
       Company
13: Courtesy of the Puerto Rico Tourism
       Company
14: Stephanie Maze/Corbis
15: Dave G. Houser/Houserstock
17: (top) Courtesy of the Puerto Rico Tourism
       Company; (bottom) Library of Congress
21: Bettmann/Corbis
23: Jose Jiminez/Primera Hora/Getty Images
24: used under license from Shutterstock, Inc.
26: Courtesy of the Puerto Rico Tourism
       Company
27: Bob Krist/Corbis
29: Franz-Marc Frei/Corbis
32: Bob Krist/Corbis
33: Courtesy of the Puerto Rico Tourism
       Company
36: A. Katz / Shutterstock.com
39: Everett Collection / Shutterstock.com
42: Hulton/Archive/Getty Images
44: Getty Images
45: Courtesy of the Puerto Rico Tourism
       Company
47: Neil Rabinowitz/Corbis
48: Tony Arruza/Corbis

CONTRIBUTORS

Senior Consulting Editor **James D. Henderson** is professor of international studies at Coastal Carolina University. He is the author of *Conservative Thought in Twentieth Century Latin America: The Ideals of Laureano Gómez* (1988; Spanish edition *Las ideas de Laureano Gómez* published in 1985); *When Colombia Bled: A History of the Violence in Tolima* (1985; Spanish edition *Cuando Colombia se desangró, una historia de la Violencia en metrópoli y provincia*, 1984); and coauthor of *A Reference Guide to Latin American History* (2000) and *Ten Notable Women of Latin America* (1978).

Mr. Henderson earned a bachelor's degree in history from Centenary College of Louisiana, and a master's degree in history from the University of Arizona. He then spent three years in the Peace Corps, serving in Colombia, before earning his doctorate in Latin American history in 1972 at Texas Christian University.

Romel Hernandez is a freelance writer and editor based in Oregon. He was born in New Jersey and graduated from Yale. He is an award-winning daily newspaper journalist who has worked in New Jersey, Colorado, and Oregon.